PREHISTORIC MO[I]

By Dr. Robert T. Bakker
Illustrated by Luis V. Rey

A Random House PICTUREBACK® Book
Random House 🏠 New York

The author and editor would like to thank Dr. Steven Stanley, University of Hawaii, for his assistance in the preparation of this book.

Text copyright © 2008 by Dr. Robert T. Bakker
Illustrations copyright © 2008 by Luis V. Rey

Visit us on the Web! www.randomhouse.com/kids

Educators and librarians, for a variety of teaching tools, visit us at www.randomhouse.com/teachers

Library of Congress Cataloging-in-Publication Data
Bakker, Robert T.
Prehistoric monsters! / by Dr. Robert T. Bakker ; illustrated by Luis V. Rey. — 1st ed.
p. cm. — (A Random House pictureback book)
ISBN 978-0-375-83945-0 (trade) — ISBN 978-0-375-93945-7 (lib. bdg.)
1. Vertebrates, Fossil—Juvenile literature. 2. Paleontology—Juvenile literature. I. Title.
QE842.B35 2008 566—dc2 2007003400

Printed in the United States of America 10 9 8 7 6 5 4 3 2 1 First Edition

I'm a paleontologist (pay-lee-uhn-TAH-luh-jist). I hunt fossils—buried remains of animals that lived long ago. Fossils tell us how the first life-forms changed into weird and spectacular creatures.

Prehistoric time is divided into "eras." The first era was the Precambrian. It started over 3 billion years ago. There weren't any animals at all during most of the Precambrian. And the only fossils come from simple seaweeds called algae.

Then something wonderful happened. . . .

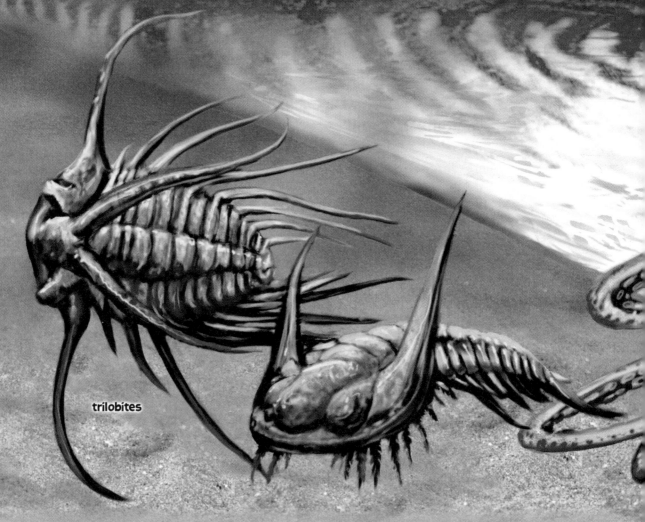

The Precambrian ended!

trilobites

The Paleozoic (pay-lee-uh-ZOH-ick) Era began about 540 million years ago. Suddenly the oceans were full of creatures with shells. The most common shelled critters had long feelers and bodies divided into three sections— trilobites (TRY-luh-bites)! The name means "three-sectioned animals."

Trilobites scurried around the sea bottom on little crab-like feet. They also swam and dug in the sand and mud.

nautiloid

YOU ARE HERE

Precambrian Paleozoic Mesozoic Cenozoic

600 500 400 300 200 100 Now
millions of years ago

Trilobite shells were suits of armor put together with hinges. Most trilobites could curl up into a ball, the way some armadillos can. And many grew horns and spikes. Why? Because trilobites had enemies—the nautiloids—who had tentacles for grabbing and jaws for crunching trilobite victims!

Pteraspis

In the Middle Paleozoic—about 400 million years ago—a new kind of monster predator appeared . . . sea scorpions! They looked like today's land scorpions but lived in salt water and grew to twelve feet long.

sea scorpion

Sea scorpions didn't have stingers. Instead, they grabbed their victims with spiked pincers and chewed them up with strong jaws that worked sideways. Many fish had to grow thick armor to protect themselves.

The earliest fish were only a foot or two long. But then—about 380 million years ago—super-sized armored fish as big as killer whales appeared! *Gorgonichthys* (gore-gun-ICK-theez) was one of the snap-headed sharks. They attacked with big fangs up front and slicing teeth in the back. Their teeth were self-sharpening and were like a pair of strong scissors.

Dinichthys

spiny shark

Gorgonichthys

Gorgonichthys had a special joint that let its entire head snap down with startling speed and force. *Gorgonichthys* would open its mouth really wide, then . . . *kee-RUNCH!*

Meanwhile, another kind of fish was doing something incredible! Over millions of years, the four fins of these fish changed into four legs, with toes for walking on land. These four-legged fish became amphibians, laying their eggs in water, frog-style. *Anthracosaurus* (an-THRACK-uh-sore-us) was an early amphibian as big as a crocodile—and just as fierce.

Amphibians couldn't go very far onto land because they needed water to breed. But then one type of amphibian changed in a very special way. It laid eggs on land, like a turtle, and became the first reptile. Now the reptiles could spread all over dry land. *Dimetrodon* (dy-MEH-truh-dahn) was a reptile that grew as big as a lion. It hunted plant-eating reptiles and big amphibians and swamp sharks with poison spines on their heads.

Dimetrodon and its kin had tall fins on their backs. The fins made the creatures look scarier. My crew is digging up *Dimetrodon* fossils right now in the red rocks of North Texas.

Anthracosaurus

YOU ARE HERE

Precambrian | Paleozoic | Mesozoic | Cenozoic

600   500   400   300   200   100   Now
millions of years ago

Dimetrodon

Edaphosaurus

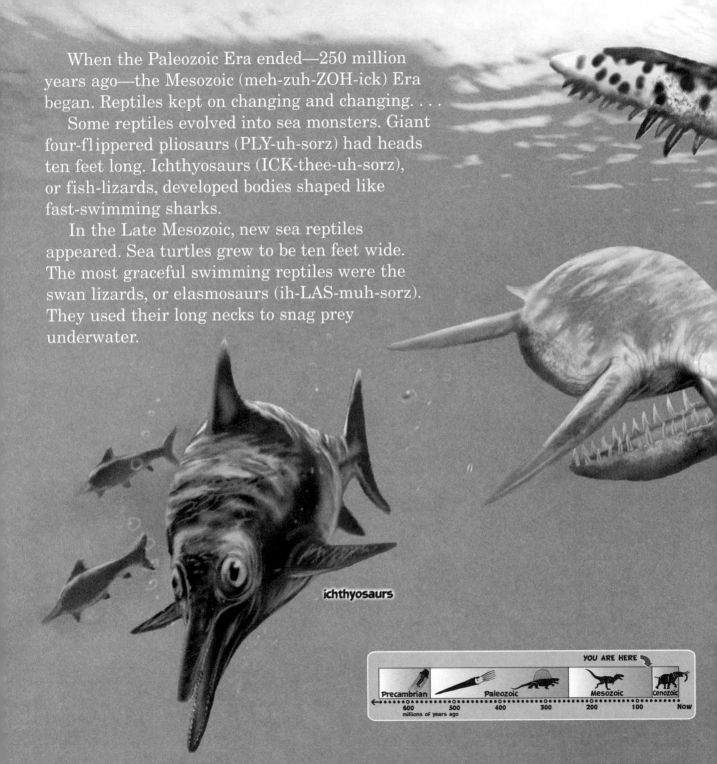

When the Paleozoic Era ended—250 million years ago—the Mesozoic (meh-zuh-ZOH-ick) Era began. Reptiles kept on changing and changing. . . .

Some reptiles evolved into sea monsters. Giant four-flippered pliosaurs (PLY-uh-sorz) had heads ten feet long. Ichthyosaurs (ICK-thee-uh-sorz), or fish-lizards, developed bodies shaped like fast-swimming sharks.

In the Late Mesozoic, new sea reptiles appeared. Sea turtles grew to be ten feet wide. The most graceful swimming reptiles were the swan lizards, or elasmosaurs (ih-LAS-muh-sorz). They used their long necks to snag prey underwater.

ichthyosaurs

YOU ARE HERE

Precambrian   Paleozoic   Mesozoic   Cenozoic

600   500   400   300   200   100   Now
millions of years ago

sea turtle

pliosaur

elasmosaur

Meanwhile, on land, another Mesozoic reptile group evolved into the most famous prehistoric monsters of all—the dinosaurs! The mighty *Tyrannosaurus rex* ran on long, strong hind legs like a giant turkey.

Many meat-eating dinos had feathers! In fact, tiny meat-eating dinosaurs evolved into birds. There were other Mesozoic fliers, too—giant pterodactyls (tehr-uh-DACK-tulz). *Quetzalcoatlus* (kwet-sul-kuh-WHAT-lus) could zoom down and scare a *T. rex*.

Tyrannosaurus rex

Anatosaurus

YOU ARE HERE

Precambrian | Paleozoic | Mesozoic | Cenozoic
600 | 500 | 400 | 300 | 200 | 100 | Now
millions of years ago

Quetzalcoatlus

baby T. rex

About 66 million years ago, the Mesozoic Era ended and the Cenozoic (seh-nuh-ZOH-ick) Era began. All the dinosaurs died out. But their little relatives, the birds, kept going.

The new rulers of the land were mammals—creatures with hair and fur. *Eobasileus* (ee-oh-buh-SILL-ee-us) was as big as an elephant and had saber teeth eight inches long, plus six horns for butting.

Eobasileus

But—surprise!—*Eobasileus* ate only plants! Its saber teeth were for fighting other *Eobasileus* and frightening meat-eaters.

waterbirds

Harpagolestes

YOU ARE HERE

Precambrian | Paleozoic | Mesozoic | Cenozoic

600 | 500 | 400 | 300 | 200 | 100 | Now
millions of years ago

In the Late Cenozoic Era—10 million years ago—there were lots of mastodons, or elephant relatives. *Platybelodon* (plaa-tee-BELL-uh-dahn) was a shovel-jawed mastodon. Its pointed upper tusks were good for fighting saber-toothed cats. The two lower tusks made a wide scoop just like a shovel!

Platybelodon

What did *Platybelodon* do with its shovel jaw?
We haven't solved that mystery yet. Maybe it
scooped up water lilies. Or dug sweet potatoes. Or
carried baby *Platybelodon* when it got tired.
    I helped dig up some shovel-tuskers in Mongolia.
Their skulls were the weirdest I've ever seen!

saber-toothed cat

YOU ARE HERE

Precambrian	Paleozoic	Mesozoic	Cenozoic

600   500   400   300   200   100   Now
millions of years ago

woolly mammoths

Later in the Cenozoic Era—3 million years ago—ice layers a mile thick spread over the land. Mammals grew heavy fur coats to stay warm.

Some elephants grew shaggy hair and became woolly mammoths. And some rhinos grew shaggy coats and became woolly rhinoceroses. Some lions grew shaggy coats, too.

There was a new predator, the most dangerous animal of all time. It didn't have fangs or claws or horns. But it was dangerously smart! Who was it? Its scientific name is *Homo sapiens* (HO-mo SAY-pee-unz).

woolly
rhinoceros

YOU ARE HERE

Precambrian   Paleozoic   Mesozoic   Cenozoic
600   500   400   300   200   100   Now
millions of years ago

Homo sapiens

It was us! Human beings! Ice Age humans made elegant spears and stone knives. And they hunted reindeer, wild horses, bears, and mammoths and made warm clothes from their hides.

YOU ARE HERE

Precambrian | Paleozoic | Mesozoic | Cenozoic

600 | 500 | 400 | 300 | 200 | 100 | Now
millions of years ago

Homo sapiens

glyptodon

Humans spread from Africa to Europe and Asia, and then to America, where they hunted giant sloths and glyptodons (GLIP-tuh-dahnz)—armadillo-like mammals as big as hippos.

Ice Age humans painted beautiful pictures of horses and bulls and rhinos on cave walls, and they carved sculptures of shaggy mammoths and buffalo.

Homo sapiens

These people were our ancestors! Our great-great-*great* . . . grandmothers and grandfathers!

I'm proud to be a descendant of those hunter-artists. I hope you are, too!